Companion to Credit Glow Up: Building Credit, Building Legacy

CREDIT GLOW UP

WORKBOOK

STEPHANIE WILLIAMS, MBA

Entrepreneur | Strategic Business Consultant | Real Estate Investor and Mentor

B&B
BOOKED & BRANDED PUBLISHING

Copyright

Published by Booked and Branded Publishing
www.bookedandbrandedpublishing.com
ISBN: 978-1-969369-05-6

To inquire about licensing, speaking, or bulk orders, contact:

📩 hello@bookedandbrandedpublishing.com

Table of Contents

Table of Contents

Welcome Letter

Dear Reader,

Congratulations on taking the bold step to not just read the book, but to actively apply it. This workbook is designed to help you:

- Turn knowledge into action
- Track your progress
- Build habits that last
- Reflect on both wins and challenges

Think of this workbook as your accountability partner. Every page you fill in is a step toward your credit glow-up and your financial future.

With strategy and consistency, you'll be amazed at how much can change in just 90 days.

— Stephanie Williams, MBA

Glow-Up Vision Statement

Write your personal vision for why you want better credit.

My Credit Glow-Up Means:

I want to stop worrying about…

____

____

____

I want to qualify for…

____

____

____

I want to feel…

____

____

____

Signature & Date: ____________________________

Building Wealth Action Plan

Record your baseline today.
Current Credit Scores (Experian / Equifax / TransUnion)

Experian:

____

Equifax:

____

TransUnion:

____

Current Debts:

____

Late Payments on File:

____

Collections/Charge-Offs:

____

My biggest challenge right now:

____

The FICO Breakdown Worksheet

FICO SCORE COMPONENTS

- Payment History – 35%
- Utilization – 30%
- Credit History Length – 15%
- Credit Mix – 10%
- New Credit – 10%

Action Steps:

My Strongest Area: ____________________________

My Weakest Area: ____________________________

One Thing I Can Improve Immediately: ____________

SECTION 1: AUDIT

Facing the Mirror Worksheet

Highlight and organize what hurts most on your report

Errors to Dispute:

Debts to Address:

Habits to Change:

SECTION 2: ACTION

Dispute Tracker

"Record every item you dispute here. Track the date sent, response received, and results so nothing falls through the cracks."

- Date Sent
- Creditor/Agency
- Issue
- Status
- Response

Sample Entries

Item	Creditor/ Agency	Date Sent	Response	Status
Medical Bill – $432	ABC Collections	07/01/2025	Pending	Open
Old Cell Phone – $215	XYZ Collections	07/05/2025	Deleted	Close
Credit Card – $1,025	Midland Funding	07/10/2025	Verified	Still Open

Goodwill Letter Template

Dear [Creditor],

I am writing regarding account ______. I acknowledge that I had a late payment in [month/year]. This was due to [brief reason]. Since then, I have maintained my account in good standing. I respectfully request that you consider removing the late mark as a goodwill adjustment.

Thank you for your consideration.

Pay-for-Delete Negotiation Notes

Use this space to log all pay-for-delete agreements. Include the creditor, negotiated amount, and confirmation details.

Collection Agency Name: ________________________

Account Number: ________________________________

Balance Offered: ________________________________

Did they agree to delete? Y / N

Confirmation received in writing? Y / N

Secured Card Plan

Bank/Issuer: ______________________________

Deposit Amount: ______________________________

Credit Limit: ______________________________

Usage Plan: ______________________________

Pay-off schedule: ______________________________

SECTION 3: ACCELERATION

Other Builder Tools Checklist

Check off each tool as you add it to your credit-building plan. These are proven strategies to establish or strengthen your profile.

- ✓ **Credit Builder Loan**
- ✓ **Chime Credit Builder**
- ✓ **Rent Reporting Service**
- ✓ **Authorized User Account**

Which will I use? ______________________________

The 30% Rule Tracker

Track your balances each month and make sure they stay under 30% of your available credit. Staying consistent here will have a major impact on your score.

(Optional note: "Pro tip: Under 10% is even better for maximum score growth.")

Account	Limit Balance	% Used	Target Balance (≤30%)
Capital One	$1,000 $250	25%	$300
Discover	$2,500 $1,200	48%	$750
Chase Freedom	$5,000 $300	6%	$1,500

Late Payment Recovery Plan

Accounts Behind: ______________________________

Minimum Payment Needed: ______________________

Date I Will Bring Them Current: ________________

Goodwill Letters to Send: _______________________

SECTION 4: MASTERY

90-Day Glow-Up Plan (Overview)

Break down your 90-day goals into weekly action steps. Use this to stay accountable and measure your progress over time.

Week 1: Pull reports, highlight errors

Week 2: Stabilize accounts (set up autopay)

Week 3: Open/build positive accounts

Week 4: Heal past mistakes (letters, disputes)

Weeks 5–12: Showcase progress + cement habits

90-Day Weekly Check-In Tracker

Come back to this page weekly to log your wins, challenges, and next actions. Consistency is where the credit glow-up really happens.

WEEK # __________

Key Actions

____

____

____

Score Changes

____

____

____

Wins

____

____

____

Challenges

____

____

____

Financial Confidence Journal

Prompt: “This week, I felt most confident about money when…”

Prompt: “One habit I practiced that made me proud was...”

Prompt: “One area I need to tighten up on is…”

Beyond the Score Reflection

With better credit, I will

The opportunities I'm excited for

One habit I will carry forward forever:

Building Wealth Action Plan

Use this checklist to build a safety net and protect your progress. Mark off each habit or account you've secured.

Emergency Fund Goal: $

___

___

___

Refinancing Opportunities:

___

___

___

Assets I want to build:

___

___

___

Who I want to help with my credit legacy:

___

___

___

Protecting My Progress Checklist

- Emergency Fund Savings
- Autopay on All Accounts
- Quarterly Credit Report Checks
- Credit Monitoring Alerts
- Accountability Partner Identified

Final Reflection & Next Steps

Pause and celebrate your progress. Write down the changes you've made and the goals you'll carry forward into the future.

My Credit Glow-Up Wins:

____

____

____

My Next 90-Day Goals:

____

____

____

Signature & Date:

____

Work With Me

Ready for deeper support? Use the link below to book your strategy session and let's build your next level together.

Want help building your business blueprint, launching your brand, or turning your knowledge into a bestselling book?

I specialize in strategy-backed ghostwriting and publishing for bold entrepreneurs who are ready to lead.

Website: www.bookedandbrandedpublishing.com
Email: hello@bookedandbrandedpublishing.com

Services:

- Ghostwriting
- Workbooks
- Publishing Support
- Business Strategy

Booking Link: [Insert Calendly or booking site]

About The Author

Stephanie Williams, MBA, is a Strategic Business Consultant, author, and powerhouse behind Booked and Branded Publishing. With over a decade of experience spanning corporate sales, real estate investment, and entrepreneurship, she brings unmatched clarity and confidence to every project.

Her expertise lies in transforming ideas into income — whether through premium ghostwriting, powerful branding, or step-by-step business building systems. Stephanie holds an MBA with a concentration in entrepreneurship from the Jack Welch Management Institute and has helped hundreds of professionals glow up their brands from the inside out.

Through her signature publishing and consulting firm, Stephanie empowers aspiring CEOs to turn their hustle into legacy — with strategy, speed, and style.

Made in the USA
Las Vegas, NV
04 November 2026

57420361R10024